THE LARGEST GLUE FACTORY IN THE WORLD

William Allen

SPUYTEN DUYVIL

New York City

Library of Congress Control Number: 2024944564

TABLE OF CONTENTS

O for God's sake
they are connected
underneath

 —Muriel Rukeyser, from "Islands"

American history is longer, larger, more various, more beautiful
and more terrible than anything anyone has ever said about it.

 —James Baldwin

Bannister's Landscapes

HAY GATHERERS

There's hayseed in the air. Bannister's not working,
having sold two Barbizon moonscapes, his day is free
from after-shaves and hair cream—Christiana's working
at her salon till six. He feels alive under cirrus clouds,
a sky that's mottled near the sea. At Purgatory Chasm
he spots grey herons in a field where hay gatherers
ease their backs, take breakfast of bread and water.
Maybe their grannies hail from Suriname, the sweat
of their brows betokens living on borrowed time.
Women scythe vetch now, others, too young to kiss,
load ox-bright carriages. In the distance, they hear
a locomotive plummet towards a setting sun. Here,
as all along the crumbling Underground Railroad,
the passing Pullman dining cars are lit by kerosene.

LEUCOTHEA RESCUING ULYSSES

This raft of Medusa is foundering off Holetown,
wrecked by the wrath of a nameless storm, 1891.
Sibyls are dirty and mud-caked, the ship's men
dead-tired, having suffered being turned to swine,
having had enough of rum, ruin, spiny mermaids
from the bottom of the sea. Twin peaks, dense
Brazilian *selvas* surface through a haze of sun
that warms a hundred years before its time.
Giant yuccas, red bananas, fan out on wetlands
freezing as an ice age pivots into place. Ulysses,
idiot-malcontent, wishes for a daughter to offer
to the gods of Euboea. Instead, the hero ravages
the sea to bargain on a white goddess, who rests
a forearm on his groin, before she takes a plunge.

COAL DOCK, EAST PROVIDENCE

It's cold at the coal dock in this land of steady habits.
Bannister's got dust in his lungs, feels bits of anthracite,
Liverpool coal, a musty blanket, burning oil, a moon
enticing tow boats towards the Seekonk shore, just
upriver from where Roger Williams, at Tockwotten,
cheered for a chaste-free deity who promised nothing
but providence. A glass of Monongahela whiskey,
his brushes poised on a shuttle bin. In the filth,
he has some hope for purity of soul, the night
casting its pall on God's creatures: farriers, Black
bootblacks, an Irish soap maker, blind in one eye,
groups of toughs shoving ladies off the sidewalk.
A calf, eaten by worms who've supped on kings.
Ursa Minor taints the sky. He wonders how or why.

RETURN OF THE HERD

How does Bannister paint light at the water's edge?
Or picture silence, printing tintypes on Dorrance Street
till noon, setting up oils, easel, in a hawk-fed meadow.
Lorries with bottled cream jostle up to Pawtucket.
Noon gives in to afternoon, shadows. Just when
he thought this tiny *pied a terre* was uninhabited,
herds return, prodded by girls with pizzle sticks,
a cattle dog nipping at the heels of every steer.
Thistles burst. Rocks, sturdy as New Brunswick's,
define distance between apprentices and the free.
A killdeer limps with a broken wing. One bull falls
behind, at the edge of this harmonic grid. Does he
paint what's not visible? Yes, Bannister, indivisible,
brushes a man into the circle of light a cow stands in.

SQUALL, BRENTON'S POINT

Lear's worst enemy couldn't have promised this storm.
Mallards bounce on eight-foot surf, take wing for shelter
on land as grave, grey cumuli descend. A ship is bound
for the Canaries, in decades past the Middle Passage,
scarcely visible as a tempest builds breath by breath.
Crashing waves along a reef: flotsam, sea foam, spurge,
a witch's cry in a rising surge. Closer, a clump of sedge
withstands the piteraq, a luna moth clinging for life
on a stalk. A white spume cast off is battered down.
Water is colored like burgoo—or crimson incense—
or a thousand starfish thrown to dunes. Exodus to
Robertsport, Monrovia, forgotten in the turbulence.
Seaweed gatherers, drenched by rain, run for cover.
The sea has no mercy. A wind howls Bannister home.

NEUTACONKANUT

Bannister hikes a hilltop when he has to get away,
once it was a serpent mound in fugitive Ohio.
Like an alienist he studies wrinkles of a brow.
How many cotton mills have burned by now?
A quadroon, a friend, were dragged to death
this day on Transit Street—Bannister escapes
to say what happened, here where an osprey
catches weasels the color of chalk. He sees
a steamship leaving Narragansett Bay, headed
for Charleston, trading in rum and molasses.
A girl named Asia spins a hoop on a basalt cliff,
everything smells like sumac. For now, sounds
from a harvest draw Bannister back to the world,
away from his picture of the restlessness of nature.

NEWSPAPER BOY

Bannister sees a waif, loafing at a cooky stand,
shouting headlines to sway a crowd into spending
pennies. Sue Wiggins, arrested for stealing a loaf
of bread, Wild Bill Hickok, dead in Deadwood,
South Dakota. Fire on a hay train. Night riders
in Nashville, Tennessee. On Weybosset Street,
all wrath is out: match girls, snake oil salesmen,
chimney sweeps, flooding a market square with
Hopkins Magic Gold Dust for thrush, two-bit
box shooks, bar-tack sewing machines, spindles,
5-cent Indian cigars, cassimere, ships' compasses,
wood pulp, women's underwear. Industry is all
as Bannister paints the boy with a stack of papers
who dreams he's David Walker, leader of free men.

BLUE HILL (NEAR BOSTON)

Bannister is lingering under a migratory flyway,
a run of minks is hiding till the fireworks stop.
Nothing stirs—not like Milk Street in the city,
the Crispus Attucks choir-boy songs and cries
of angels emblazoning the earth. No sachems
at the creek swell—only a mill wheel on a river
turning mud into muck—a paradise of squash,
gin shacks, rum holes, teetotalers. Remember
when Christiana lay lifeless in the snow as if
to rest forever? Candlelight dims, grim, chill.
Bannister's as poor as Job's turkey, with horse
and buggy to reach Blue Hill. July is coming—
cicadas trill—his only thoughts are to quash
the war drums from the shadow of the trees.

DUTCH COW, GIRL, MEADOW

He stops at Kaaterskill to paint clouds as they loom
above the Hudson, on his return from Philadelphia,
the Centennial, where his "Under the Oaks" won
bronze, where museum guards refused to see him.
He's "colored" on the train, even when his palette
won't favor black or white. He loved "The Death
of Cleopatra," a pomological display, a massive,
wheeling Corliss engine, a cricket match, a peek
at the Hermit Kingdom of Korea. A day crazily
smelling of rhododendrons. Reconstruction was
a sham. Transcendentalists are mute and few
now speak about emancipation. A Dutch cow,
a girl, a meadow—they are the hues of humankind,
with a sky like the sea of Bannister's beloved home.

ROWBOAT IN A STORM

He's somewhere off Porcupine Island, a crayon study
shows Georges Bank, where his mother raised him.
In his sloop *Fanchon*, he nears the coast of Eden,
Maine, of landlocked spermaceti works, a cyclops
cave where an ocean's offal bakes. Winds come up,
he reefs sail, comes to. At 93 Benevolent, Bannister
splotches paint, eats canned eggs, cranks the phone
to speak to Gustine Hurd from the Ann-Eliza Club,
who lectures him on life in the year 2000, when four
towers beam light across the city and Freetown girls
balloon-sail to the coliseum at Roger Williams Park.
He's happy with plum pudding, wine or pepper pot,
because—as he looks again—an indistinct something
in his painting stirs, emerging in mystical fog and dark.

THE DRINKING POOL

Perhaps he too is a shade, as he turns to speak with people
lingering at an opening. Bannister stands in the pavilion, but
Garrison and Bronte look straight through him, now that
the wars are over, a fight for equal rights is done. What has
been won? Bannister has a private studio, the leisure time
to paint; Christiana, her Madame Carteaux Hair Doctress
shops and her society. The drinking pool, as he captures it,
is bottomless, feeding creatures of a world that fly at night
to siphon bison blood or goats' gall when it's still. A fire-
hot sun sets over a pond of evergreens. His Lisbon baker
cries *saudade*, longing for a place that isn't anywhere, a state
of mind that can't be bought, but in the meadow he tries
to paint before evening falls. A lark lets out a single note
as if to say, he would have made out poorly if not for her.

for Jesse Murry

ROAD TO A HOUSE WITH A RED ROOF

Circus tents along a road to Taunton, Massachusetts,
three dancing bears. Bannister relaxes, closes his eyes
to hear the ocean. Circassian Black Sea beauties, true
Caucasians for a world to see. Barnum's baby beauty
contests, a blue gazelle, Schlitzie the Monkey Girl
and his sister Athelia in a sidecar, the "Nondescript"
(or "missing link"), beluga whales brought from Isle
au Coudres in water tanks on wagons that stopped
in every hamlet on the turnpike to New York City.
Light-box panoramas of the West, an Orang-Outan.
Barnum noisily brings picture shows, Bannister just
wants to sketch the countryside and cows, a feeling
rising from his ribs to his hands to a canvas, a hint
of his temper in the guise of a road, a house and trees.

LOOKING EAST FROM THE HOMEOPATHIC HOSPITAL

Bannister sets up under a birch in Snowtown—all torn up
by rioting as if it was Hardscrabble, where drunken sailors
with guns mowed down a congregation. There's a shrine
for the War between the States, a memorial for heroes,
for officers of the 54th Infantry. Back then, this would
have been Election Day, a King Coromantee would be
rapping people's shins with a bastinado. That's passed,
what dignity there is comes from civic pride. He walks
to Planet Street, talking to stevedores from Stockholm,
promising portraits before their trip to Guinea. Bannister
listens to a song of a granddad to his little boy, as they
share stories of Boa Vista. Looking east from the hospital,
Bannister eyes a river flowing towards the sea, a continent
beyond the coast, the motherland he can only dream about.

TWILIGHT, WILLOWS, SHEEP

On Candlemas, Bannister calms Christiana's fears of dying
penniless, of spiders in the trundle bed, broken windows,
an icy pond till the middle of March. Come spring, they'll
amble in rugosa rose, hear towhees in the woods or owls
at Sachuest, where a rock-face silhouette resembles Cato,
the ships' cook he knew on a ship they called the *Venus*.
Later they'll sit in fields or sift through harvest aftermath
of corn husks, pumpkin, rue, dill—bones of a coyote kill.
Queen Anne's lace, a kettle pond, kingfishers with a carp.
It's a stone's throw to the roadside quarry on a day when
he will not paint but pray that it won't be him that sleeps
beneath a stone until the day when everyone's set free.
Dairy farms are dark as they reach a headland by the sea.
Shepherds fan out, looking for a sheep that's lost its way.

The Largest Glue Factory
in the World

The magic of the street is the mingling of the errand and the epiphany.

—Rebecca Solnit, *Wanderlust: A History of Walking*

When knowledge will cover the earth like water covers the sea

—Peter Cooper

A WALK THROUGH BLISSVILLE

I walk in furrows that once were farmers' fields,
searching for tree ferns. A lapsed Baptist cleric
shoos me from an orchard as a November sun
sets beyond her apple trees. I breathe in lichen,
liken today to a 15th Ward Smelling Committee's
punt up Newtown Creek to catalog the odors.
Maybe I'll see a raven as we motor up channel,

or turkeys, like I saw on a treeless boulevard
in Staten Island near the Fresh Kills landfill.
I dream of offal, garbage scows plowing up
Blissville cul-de-sacs to toss out carriage nags.
I pass deserted lots, clock factories, potholes
on the LIE, looking for friends, a place to find
some solace to lessen the stress of the stench.

BLACK-CROWNED NIGHT HERON

Up English Kills, a wading bird has stabbed an eel
below the glassy surface. Cries from the Schamonchi,
a ferry with a dumpster swimming pool, where weeds
keep channel worms alive. Furman's Island housed
the largest glue factory in the world, Peter Cooper's
tanning works before it moved upstate to Gowanda,
where its cookhouse sludge still pollutes Lake Erie.

Here fish are boiled to isinglass for paper and beer,
cow collagen is made into chairs, violins and Jell-O.
Way off in the distance, the Chrysler Building juts
out from behind a sewage plant. Turpentine, azo
dye, methane in the aquifer, where no otters play
by waterfront lots. It's the night heron that patrols
the creek for shiners that draws us here each night.

THE ENDLESS CHAIN

I smell sulfur in the wind off toadfish salt flats.
Cord grass, mud snails, a whiff of conch decay.
These were tidal mills before a Brooklyn barge
crossed. We ground corn at Mill Basin, upriver
in Bushwick, by breweries, pigsties and timber
stores built by Peter Cooper's saw-tooth chain.
I dream of lug nuts for mechanical advantage,

to propel El trains up Third Avenue as they
drip creosote on pushcarts and locomotives
down below, while chain boats slowly steer
the rivers. I keep inventing tools in my sleep,
contraptions to do the heavy lifting, like the
American language unburdening, like endless
chains of our relations, hauling us on, forever.

AT SUNFISH POND

Mist rakes the sky by Kalustyan's in Little India,
long gone are New York Harlem Railroad horses,
the elms or kissing bridge I seek out for my love
who's arrived in purple sweatpants from Berlin.
I try to lure her to my lair, where the cattle pens
and farmsteads at 28th and Fourth once thrived,
where Bowery gangs would stock the abattoirs

and charnel houses for Peter Cooper's glue.
Here buttonwood and fields of clover grew,
a high tide rising in brackish Sunfish Pond,
now a Blimpie by the Morgan Library. I tell
you I smell licorice or spell "licorice," I don't
know which, wandering from Rolling Rock
to Ravenswood, as if I was the god of travel.

TORPEDOES

There are shanty towns at Gravesend, for deck hands
and hungry Scots. Peter Cooper used Fort Hamilton
for piloting his torpedo, a gift to Greece for its war
against the Turks. Catboats ply the Narrows, a crew
arrives the day that Byron died. He uses grapeshot
cannon to furnish steam for the vessels plunging
into the lower bay. Oyster dredges test a blast, six

miles out, a Panama freighter mangles the wires
he steers with, the whole mess sinks. His boat is
found without a bomb on board. No one notes
beneath the waves that a million catfish wander,
oblivious to American good will. A slanting rain,
a push forward—recalling the words of Farragut
saying "Damn the torpedoes, full steam ahead."

TRANSATLANTIC CABLE

You never knew when news would come. It took months
to hear of the defeat at Waterloo, that a child died in Bath.
The War of 1812 might not have been if an envoy sailed
on time. A cable laid between St. John's and Nova Scotia,
a line played out across the mid-Atlantic, a knotted cord
above Atlantis, where giant squids held sway or crawled
above a sink hole in the earth. Not far from the Azores,

a cable snaked from Heart's Content to Foilhommerum,
a Gaelic isle of grazing cattle, where news got through.
Slavers sailed both ways, Victoria sent a wire to James
Buchanan, at 0.1 words per minute, of mutual esteem.
Peter Cooper profited, just as his steel mills sot the sky
with acid. Too many volts did in the transatlantic cable,
but I give thanks for it now, as I text my friend in Perth.

AT JAMAICA BAY

A paradise of glossy ibises! Even in April, as ice grips
reed grass, terns congregate. If I was a body of water,
I'd be Jamaica Bay, where a Saab is ditched in slush,
an old piano sits mid-channel. I trudge in flurries with
my daughter, who'd rather be at Bell House in Gowanus
for an indoor barbecue. And hundreds of moths appear
and some say it would have made a great world harbor.

Railroads bought all shipping rights-of-way, and a cross-
borough parkway kept it as undeveloped swamp. I like
its relative obscurity, a gem despite its half-dead oyster
beds, a rush of jets, dilapidated fish oil fertilizer farms.
Fields of kale, urban rangers spearing Styrofoam at will.
Clouds of countless pigeons, a rotten dinghy. Not even
Peter Cooper saw its worth, despite his plans for progress.

PUBLIC READING ROOM

For a dog, there are countless scents in the city, but for
me to isolate just one or two can test my flair for what
our atmosphere is made of. Here it's anise, pine, I think.
On my way to the homeless shelter where I often sleep,
I stop for a book at Cooper Union, once the only public
reading room for working folks when arson, draft riots,
great awakenings consumed the land. It's musty tomes

of *Saturday Evening Post, Blackwood's, Aristotle's Masterpiece,*
students thumbing *Popular Mechanics, Architectural Review.*
Once it even had a gallery of Christian art, with Titians,
Leonardo's *St. John Weeping* and Canaletto's landscapes.
I shop for corn flakes, no-pulp orange juice for the men.
Bernard wants to talk about Vietnam. Later, to snoring,
smelly feet, I grab a bunk, curl up with Edward Bellamy.

HENRY RED CLOUD AT THE GREAT HALL

I'm Henry Red Cloud of Pine Ridge, South Dakota.
My people get by these days under the sun or moon
by turning to the stars for light above the Badlands.
The town's hit bottom, awash in burgers, lung-rot
and tequila. In a dream, my namesake Red Cloud
returns to the hills, gives me the eagle quill I wear
tonight, generations after he stood here, as I accept

a prize at Cooper Union, for land that's carbon free.
Grandfather said back then he'd no longer fight, that
we should work with pale-face pioneers, like Lincoln,
Clinton and Obama. Now I bring solar to the health
of the Black Hills, so the Sioux can be free of toxins
in the Cheyenne River, to bring back forgotten songs
of spirit animals who teach us to live our lives as one.

PLANTS OF MANHATTAN

My friend James exhibits flowers from the Arctic,
the ones that grow in Brooklyn, those that
are native, not invasive. North of Harlem,
near Spuyten Duyvil, I find a cache of flora
dating to the Pleistocene. Amaranth, colic root,
asters, meadow zizia, Jesuit's bark, widowsfrill,
chickweed, huckleberry, an ipecac that sprouts

at my knee. We've hit upon New Jersey tea
like Peter Cooper used to brew, kinnikinnick,
prickly bog sedge, not to mention scaldweed.
Azure bluet and leeks in a ravine, swamp pink,
cabbage, spread out in shafts of light. Orange
grass, even moonseed. I identify a lot of plants
but wonder if there isn't buttercup or juniper.

RINGWOOD MANOR

No one lives here now, but the portico and grounds
are full of spirits. Runaway slaves and some Lenape
indentured, a hundred years deceased, sweep porches
where they see the ghost of Aaron Burr, wandering alone,
while a revolutionary mapmaker sits with a compass
chewing pemmican in the rising fog. Rochambeau's
army, in unmarked graves, whispers *the Marseillaise*.

By a patio, a patch of cool air intrudes at tea time
with a scent of lavender, no one knows why, save
to say it's the lady of the manor. At an ironworks,
the magnetic center of Passaic, stink wafts up out
of slag heaps, raccoon bones and Indian tobacco.
Here Peter Cooper's realm raked in raw materials,
a trail of leavings, his voice still shrill in the quarry.

AT PENNY BRIDGE

We take a cab to Calvary Cemetery, in memory
of girls who died of cholera, exhumed at night,
ferried from Manhattan to this rural tract where
the dead are restless or stirring in Gothic plots.
We walk by elms, evergreens, climb a hill to pick
toadstools in a glen. We want to smell the lilacs
in the wind, where ancient chimneys stand and

we can lie in fields of phlox bursting into bloom.
We row to abandoned islands of industrial decay,
discover graves where all the clocks have stopped.
Purple finches mob in a potter's field, at the closed-
down Penny Bridge station, where mourners come
in droves. We loiter on a rise to glimpse a far-off
clutch of towers in the town, glinting in the sunset.

BISHOP'S RING

A painter sits in a locust grove, mixing his spirits
for rendering a sky, to try and capture the eerie
fallout of an eruption. He's never been to Java
and is not keen to travel. But there's afterglow
from Krakatau that sits as ash on windowpanes.
There's a blue-brown ring around the sun today
that drives mechanics out to stoops on Broadway.

The smallest variation in the pivot of the Earth
sends animals, adventurers, to climb new heights
on mountains sliding to the sea. The last quagga
died as the slave trade collapsed in Great Britain,
the Orient Express connecting Paris to Bucharest.
When will the sunsets pale? The azure halo augurs
an end to a machine age and beckons new horizons.

A HISTORY OF THE NEWTOWN CREEK

I'm taken by this seaway dredged for coal boats:
the smell of linseed oil, the smell of tarpaulin,
the smell of hyacinth, burning rubber, wax,
the smell of car exhaust, pig iron and pine,
the smell of squalor, diapers, dogwood, sex,
the smell of fins and fishnet, arugula, Shiraz,
the smell of eucalyptus, locusts, lemon rind.

The smell of boiling bones, salt or pickle brine,
the smell of goldenrod, car fumes, rotten fruit,
the smell of gelatin, hair gel, fresh-baked bread,
the smell of gunpowder, oak-hewn hulls, the dead
the smell of tar, mud flats, peat moss, gasoline,
the smell of tiredness, dog-scent, autumn wind,
the oldest channel to thread a fragrant riverside.

Crossing Queensbridge

Under thy shadow by the piers I waited;
Only in darkness is thy shadow clear.
The city's fiery parcels all undone,
Already snow submerges an iron year...

—Hart Crane, "To Brooklyn Bridge"

Remember, and remember always, that all of us, and you and I especially,
are descended from immigrants and revolutionists.

—Franklin Delano Roosevelt

PROLOGUE—BRIDGES

A bridge connects two continents,
a lorry crossing with figs
from the Golden Horn.

Chenyang spans the restless Linxi,
where white storks
settle in the reeds.

Tagus, at Alcántara, carried Roman soldiers
and their oxen
on moonless nights.

Red Python, in the city
of forgotten dreams, links fishwives
to Borneo Island.

Charles Bridge, on the Vltava,
houses palindromes
and curses of the gentry.

A double-helix bridge
in Singapore gives runners
access to the city islands.

Langkawi, in the land
of a thousand bridges,
takes walkers up Mat Cincang.

Puente de Mujer in Buenos Aires
is packed with stalling
motorbikes today.

6th October looks out over
the dirty Nile
where pleasure boats abound.

Ponte Vecchio boasts pilgrims
marching to Fiesole
to avoid bubonic plague.

Al-Sarafiya, across the Tigris,
lies partially under water
and collapsed.

Gabriel Tucker, dry, dusty,
links United Nations Drive
to Providence Island.

Glienicker Brücke is a fog-bound
conduit for spies, prisoners,
from East Berlin.

A bridge is yet to be built
to Sicily, where only sky
looms over a wine dark sea.

CROSSING QUEENSBRIDGE

This is my ode to a drab-brown bridge of fear
and wonder, its two-deck cantilevered spans
of nickel steel are a topsy-turvy Eiffel Tower,
its struts thrown down by a wandering giant
with a foot on Blackwell's Island. Rays of sun
catch eyebar filigree. Owls Head sludge boats
pass by with our intestines, as Esther Truong
of Saigon pushes empty shopping carts uphill.
The bridge is an act of love and usury, a band-
aid on a century of forgetting. We trade coins
on the upper level, with imps, impostors and
inventors, enjoying the physics of its motion.
A signal from heaven for what comes next:
I brake, feet down, the bridge begins to shake.

RAVENSWOOD

From here you see the truss half-finished,
suspended in air, a bridge to the beyond.
Camels come, a herd of Asian elephants,
a father, leading kids on a day crusade,
in a storm of locusts on a gritty trestle.
Hairy oxen, a parade of pickle trucks,
taxis, Ho-Ro flatbeds, log long-haulers,
freighters with things like wheel-wells,
hand-blown glass, rebar, rolled oats,
horse dung, coil springs, hair gel, beet-
root, sugar cane, mint mouthwash,
armored cars, rubies, Kashmiri spices,
seaweed, sable hats, tarantulas, a steady
flush of offal, leaf mold, Asian bird flu.

REPAIR DOCKS, GOWANUS

William Chase paints *plein air* at repair docks,

the fog lifting in a sky that blanches lumber

not fit for hurricanes. Barges clog the basin

where hickory trees came down last night.

Dinghies line the docks, soap tins, rusted

benches, smelling salts, sulfur and an axe.

A dolphin swims to Ninth Street Bridge,

drinks in the lye from a tannery trash pit.

Linseed oil and encaustic add to a mess

of bristle and ink, this ringing in my ears.

Hostlers sneak down Brooklyn streets

as I strain to make out a harmonium, as

if it may detect a surge of bluefish darting

across the bay where there is beauty, rest.

TROLLEY STOP, MIDNIGHT

Footballers snatch a Guatemalan flag
on a ramp of the Queensboro Bridge,
winds unleashed in churning waters,
petrels riding thermals in the clouds.
Minnows dart in pools of motor oil,
Xi'an dhows sailing for Botany Bay.
Atlantic herring, scrod, are racing to
the sea. Grizzled Adam Purple, out
of Alphabet City, rides a cargo trike
with a macaw, aiming for meat scraps
in Blissville. Newsboys lug *Korean Times*
on tuk-tuks. Divas with flutes perform
as coal barge crews reach Hell Gate, as
oystercatchers open urchins in a marsh.

FERRY LANDING

At the ferry landing, lots of iron ore, deck paint,
flywheels, water troughs that fed old fish farms.
My life is an oil spill—Deepwater, Amoco Cadiz,
tankers carrying the dead and those who worked
on Wall Street. A jail boat rests at Rikers, a tram
sparks up, guard dogs training for aerial sorties.
Underwater turbines near Hallet's Cove whisper
what we're thinking: the stars are shifting south...
I look over to a dog park, where Boston Whalers
dock to load off crystal meth. Voyages, we've all
had them, but now we rest at the river's bottom.
After storms, the bridge is packed with joggers,
now there's not a soul on the east side bike path,
just a Moran tug shunting a barge of coal upriver.

ON BLACKWELL'S ISLAND

Kahnawake workers helped build the bridge
with cofferdams and caissons, chords that
loom by Louis Kahn's Four Freedoms Park,
a grey, decommissioned ship without a keel.
Once the Panama Canal was done, Jamaican
riveters came to fix the bridge, shopping on
Pear Avenue. Now called Roosevelt Island,
its shadows drown the streets, as simulated
shrieks of hawks scare subway passengers.
Soon plants grown hydroponically will take
the place of smallpox sickbay ruins. Below,
bateaux go by unnoticed, pike swim north,
otters after mussels drift by clanging buoys.
Gold tips on spires are warding off witches.

WORLD TOWN

Bridge of tyranny, lust and longing, a graffiti tag
reads *World Town* but all I can smell is marijuana.
A lady with a painless limp is dangling on a parapet,
reaching skyward in disarray, searching for closure
while hustlers head for Corona, Rego Park, Floral
Gardens or the tombstone row at Mount Calvary.
A panel van has a giant fortune cookie on its roof.
I walk the bridge each day with others, looking for
a loft where Hart Crane's father cooked up candy.
White roofs, cool roofs, urban heat effect stirs up
a torrid breeze and one long, steam train whistle,
monkeys vaulting in a wild-grape treetop canopy.
Sheep graze by the bulwarks men are shoring up,
as they prepare for the hurricane that's on its way.

SOCCER OCTAGON

Kids wait for ice cream in the shade of a yew.
A goalie kicks a ball that lifts in a Nor'easter,
sails over the city and beyond an orange buoy.
Gulls wheel on army helicopter down-drafts,
by mule towpaths of the FDR, where hospital
window glass refracts a burn center's wounds
and rain seeps down in sucking eddies of grief.
Spittle bugs crowd the bus route, horse loops
winding around and past the Lighthouse Park.
We love the known unknowns, a briar patch,
the soccer octagon, a phantom toll gate and
hunchback Quasimodo reading comic books.
From here, you can just make out a chicken
coop in Queens, hens scratching in the dust.

A HISTORY OF CHEWING GUM

It starts with a sapodilla tree in Yucatan,
a factory for making toys and auto tires.
The thing to do was chew while dancing
on a Model T assembly line or ambling
past Saks Fifth Avenue in search of hats.
The American Chicle Company began
in LIC, not far from the Montauk cutoff.
Once cows mustered at a water trough
near the bridge's keystone, by a Sunday
farmers' market off Hog Island, where
boars ran wild and boys skipped school
to dream of laughing hobos, a lost sailor
lunching on his eggs and shandy—and
bubble gum for every sucker in the land.

MOUNT VERNON HOTEL AND GARDENS

Abigail Adams slept here once in taffeta, now
under a trestle of the bridge, son John Quincy
too, as they smoked, tossed quoits, wrote notes
with quill pens under a larch where I lie tonight.
At Kip's Bay, there's a tower for dropping lead
to mold a musket ball, as President Jefferson did
when the fur trade thrived and big-boned fossils
belonged to giants of the earth. Later chimneys
came, and kids playing stickball at Sutton Place.
Before the bridge, tram and subway lines, it may
have been a pasture paradise, a trotting course
with orchards, boxwoods, lilacs, ferns or willow.
Sycamores stood close to where we lay in grass
and avowed our love, as if there was no tomorrow.

MAISON TROPICALE

I did a double take to see Maison Tropicale
(of Brazzaville, in Congo) here by the bridge,
a prefab, flat-pack house from the architect
of airplanes, as if in colonial Pointe-Noire,
where bats, bee-eaters, swifts and hoopoes
fly in a forest crown. The houses multiplied
(London, Niamey, Kinshasa), I visited each
one, well-designed, inexpensive, built to last,
I rode an overland express to avoid a rapids
on the river that I took to come back home.
But here it's Christie's auction house who's
put it on the market for a cool five million.
Maison Tropicale, set up by my house, sold
to the highest bidder, come hell, high water.

HALLETT'S COVE, 2057

We see what's left of the relics of the bridge,
years after its collapse into the polluted river.
Oyster beds teem along the shore, as bright
and clear as the day three ships first sailed
these Narrows. Kids kick about in hot tubs,
a suspension bike trail slopes up past Turtle
Bay to a public school for the dispossessed.
Dragonfly towers support new vertical farms
with laborers from Maldives, Mexico. Storms
wrack the Pacific Rim, an elfin animism lives
as clerics, scribes, hide in underground caves.
Crows, flamingos, sharks are long since gone,
as well as elephants, pandas and solitary bees.
But the Khaju Bridge in Isfahan is brightly lit.

FOR DINK'INESH (LUCY)

Tens of Ethiopians, trained on Mount Entoto,

sprint to a trolley stop atop the Queensbridge,

as if they were back at home where women

walk with bales of eucalyptus on their heads,

as they did as *Australopithecus afarensis,* foraging

for food, fruit, nuts or seeds in the open bush

or woodlands where I sit tonight, hungry for

khat and coffee, *fir-fir, injera,* lemon-flavored

Ambo from the Great Rift Valley. We stay

at the Andromeda Hotel in Addis Ababa,

working on a global information system for

the stars, for myriad, beeping satellites that fix

positions on runners, who, after bottled water,

sail on past to clinch the New York Marathon.

TREES

Up here I dream to reach the northern forest,
while under the bridge, eels pass tons of water
through their guts on their journey to the gulf.
Up here, I see the city as from a giant conifer.
Right beside me, a cable car is passing, a man
who looks like me when I was twenty staring
out, lost in reverie, a flood of consciousness,
picturing a labyrinth of crooked trees. Seawall
traps the tide as workers on a barge begin to
fill in piers, the bridge's fretwork, truss chords
straining, a ferry leaving from a Harlem dock
steers wide, towards Lake Tear of the Clouds,
the Hudson's source, where in the hardwoods
brown bear cubs are greedily devouring trout.

21 Stations

If you're transferring to a bus to LaGuardia Airport,
good luck! I hope you make your flight.

—Awkwafina, IRT Flushing Line 7-train announcement

TIMES SQUARE

I'm sitting on a 7 train, penciling amoebas, mocking
up a print set called "Three Worlds." Sleepy tourists
drift past parked cars, by an army recruiting booth
under a spiral of stars, where three roads meet.
Today there are no pipe bombs or happy carolers
from *Les Miserables*, there are no soldiers' families
to spread a word of peace for the Middle East.

Here's a fish lung of the city, as Yoko Ono
likes to say, where we hide till we forget--
nearby is an Odditorium, *The Lion King*.
My daughter's clocked out as an usher
at a Dead Sea Scrolls exhibit—I smile
to recall our hike high in the Judean Hills,
waiting for Moses and Aaron. Broadway's

auctions feature rifles, rice wine, rigatoni.
There's an afterglow where Hamilton was
musket-balled by Burr, tugboats riverside,
sun rising over the Big Duck of Flanders,
Shinnecock men out oystering North Sea.
Today I'll ride this subway line, beside me
in the car a Sri Lankan boy reads Nietzsche.

BRYANT PARK

In the subway, dioramas of the Eocene mask
a sea of wires, an Ethernet, where I'm pushed
by passengers, panhandlers, all who ponder
thoughts of sleep. People speed-walk, not any
two colliding as they race to make their trains.
Magpies perch above the public library, where
I linger with a stack of books and manuscripts,

including *Gilgamesh*, Sappho, *Lyle the Crocodile*,
Go, Dog, Go! I've got *The Flowers of St. Francis*
to speak to crows, a *Red Book Guide to Queens*
and every book by J. M. Coetzee, each which
brings a chill that breaks across the boulevard.
My ocean lighthouse, my library of Alexandria,
I love you like a lamb, a labyrinth, a portico,

your cabinets of curiosity eternally on view.
It's here I sleep away time's tapping, near
Teepee Town where souvenirs were sold
to crowds that mobbed an automat, sots
doling out party hats on New Year's Eve.
As my train moves off towards Flushing,
I've got my book of maps on Archenland.

GRAND CENTRAL

Battling trucks, Twitter, truth and *joie de vivre*,
I catalog cacophony as it scatters into dust,
the scrolls of acorn and oak leaf ornaments,
an Internet of Things: a son's pocket watch,
a lilac necktie, an almanac, a cricket in a cage.
This is Grand Central, a tribute to Palladio,
Nick Cave, a parliament of fools, a teething

one-year old, a keeper of the rocks, a shy
commuter out of Rye who's come too late.
On Platform 47, we hear counter-fugues,
a girl's barrette gives off smells of smoke.
Remember concourse backlit signboards,
with jungle landscapes or the Plain of Jars
with its desiccated desert palms, mangoes,

cottages under a Rio rainbow sunset? Now
I'm Mercury, slayer of dogs, god of traffic,
thieves, temptations, lost in a maze of foot
and hoof, straphangers queuing for a 7:42,
gawkers outside a tobacco shop and hawks
circling at the Daily News. A sudden lurch,
our local rolls into the river of forgetfulness.

VERNON—JACKSON AVENUES

Train cars shoot out of the Steinway Tunnel,
screech to a halt by my favorite cafe, sumacs
at the Newtown Creek where cats in cubbies
dream of forest fires along a lake. We pass
the wreckage of a lorry full of peanut oil,
oats, cargo rice on barges buffeted by wind,
a band of mariachis humming *Cielito Lindo*.

Women flash playing cards, muttering oaths
below the elevated tracks where lovers kiss,
dreaming of Baucis and Philemon, as beech
and linden intertwine despite a god's rebuke.
An urban nature trail has fossils, I consider
 a theology of sky and pools of orange dye.
We see dram boats hug the coast, a dolphin

who's lost her compass, nosing up the river.
We stop for tea, a girl in frog boots doodles,
we see in orbit Kwangmyŏngsŏng-3 (Bright
Lode Star), a satellite sent up by South Korea,
where lynx still rule the DMZ. Nests of paper
wasps, a water tower boasting *Save the Palestine*.
As we pass, the Pulaski bridge is drawing open.

HUNTERS POINT

We strap-hang in the fastest-growing borough,
past sand lots, salt ponds and Arbitration Rock.
Lost in our devices or secret searches, we turn
on a long curve of a 7 train as it veers to P.S.1,
twin spires, a dim charcuterie, a fancy beer hall,
stone cemeteries and a gurgling sawtooth creek.
We gaze at a many-windowed biscuit factory,

a Swingline Staples, a Breyer's ice cream sign,
billboards crumbling by Sunnyside train yards.
We take in the Tom Cat Bakery, the birth of
each loaf of rye, every hand-me-down cake
or nut croissant a call to end world hunger.
We spy cantilever trusses of the 59th Street
Bridge, dream butterfly farms of 2030, eked

out of back-lot peas, watercress, cabbage,
radishes, tomatoes, carrots, kale and kelp.
We watch the freighters *Cherokee, Adriatic,*
bound for seal pup slaughter in the north.
We thirty pilgrims get set to ride the train
past 5 Pointz and its street art, with none
of the wounds of the canal across the river.

COURT SQUARE

At Court Square, we stop at artists' studios,
one with paintings of Queens Street names:
Farmers Boulevard, Palermo Street, Utopia
Parkway, Linnaeus Place and Jagger Lane.
I listen on the fly to bits of the 167 tongues
that are spoken here, ask for alms, excuse
lies, beg pardon, share my lifelong passions.

I overhear the local folklore, where a boy
goes hunting for ancient rocks, discovering
a granite outcrop at Twelfth and 43rd where
smashed-in, freight line flatcars come to die.
Where Mispat squaws once seined the shoal
for shad or sturgeon, I kayak on Arbor Day,
tip over into the creek, squelch into bones

of one relative, Eliphalet Nott, a minister
who turned this shoreline into capital, sold
off lots for gin joints and caulk distributors.
Starfish creep by dockside carts of melons.
At Court Square we stop to breathe, unsure
what a few Tokyo soloists are up to, as we
lurch from one side of the river to the other.

QUEENSBORO PLAZA

Our Auckland nurse drinks sparkling water,
musing on death-by-fire and Jet Blue signs.
Across a platform from our curious crowd,
a bride in a flowery dress takes photos for
her *abuelo* in Honduras, of family, factories
for horse-drawn carriages or fighter planes.
Beyond the bike lane, fields of yellow tulips,

the arc of Q trains bending towards Astoria.
A tractor excavates a block for Quality Inn,
parakeets are perched in an Asian pear tree.
Shearwaters circle the bridge before a storm,
our crew sips beer, like logical philosophers,
thinking of islands on the moon, wondering
why fireworks won't bring fame, till a 7 train

arrives and we continue to the east, high heels
catching on cracks in pavement. Fire engines
shriek. The Catalan composer and Hollis cop
take turns nagging the urban anthropologist,
as he's undercharged us for our six-hour tour.
We settle up, head off towards Aviation High,
the air is thick with smells of Turkish coffee.

33RD STREET—RAWSON STREET

We descend an ornate, Roman viaduct, keyed
to traffic on the boulevard of death, as a taxi
heads for Aqueduct and spews out gritty soot,
enough fumes for my yearly carbon footprint.
We hear minor scales fluttering from a condo
window, where a child saws away at mazurkas
of Scriabin. At the high school, teens crank up

a Cessna Mescalero for senior projects. We fall
into a single file past sugar shacks, a botanica,
to reach a Belfast pub for burgers and a black
and tan—before we seek the bamboo garden.
We love the paradise of Sunnyside, a utopia
for bees. Two of the travelers are tired, but
joke with our city archaeologist (his 'career

lying in ruins'), as he shaves a stick, leads us
to blueberry bushes, locusts, trees-of-heaven.
We visit a rooftop farm that's growing beets,
basil and rhubarb beside its panoramic view.
On Skillman Avenue, dahlias are in bloom,
someone's fixed a flat on a fruit truck, cups
clink in a courtyard that we may never reach.

40TH STREET—LOWERY STREET

We go through stations without stopping, famous
for weed walks where burdock, spurge, mulberry
and lungwort grow in easements by McDonald's,
where a wrestling club once stood when Ronnie,
our librarian, was seventeen and eager for a prom.
We fix our attention inwards or on civil engineers
who plot post-plastic for the district as a pinnacle

of progress. Subway workers wear orange vests,
with drills for track repair in hand, dream of tar
on faraway bridges. Monks chat with a masseuse,
then questions come: on 9/11, where were you?
One was in the towers—now an angel in heaven,
a mother glued to a phone, connected to no one,
an artist running into flames as a wave of people

gather others, while now she eyes our subway
passengers to sketch: a female bodybuilder,
a prodigal daughter, a copyist without a job,
a host of weary travelers holding onto poles.
Mets fans chatter their way to a double header,
men read *El Diario, China Press* or the *Irish Echo.*
We race on gaily towards foxes in Forest Park.

46TH STREET—BLISS STREET

Our Dakar banker has never been to Woodside,
he says that it feels like dormitory towns at home,
with textiles, plywood, processed foods or cocoa,
all but wooden carvings and a sea at the equator.
We walk along footpaths to a graveyard, where
countless bodies got dug up, ferried, re-buried,
clearing the land for factories, clothing shops,

steam pumps, carriages, kerosene and coal.
Our vet says there are more dead than living,
have they understood the changing landscape?
We make a stop at Triangle 54, a shrine to all
the wars, to our domestic and foreign sacrifice.
We pass a stile by Ruhe's Wild Animal Farm,
what's left of its exotic spa, a vaccination hub

for imported beasts, a cargo stop for Barnum
and Bailey, for American circuses and zoos,
for pythons, rhinos, for Hashish the Camel
of Coney Island's "Streets of Cairo," tapirs,
a pyramid of Pomeranians, a talking crow.
We're awed by the wonder, violence, greed
of this worn-out spot we call a global village.

52ND STREET—LINCOLN AVENUE

Some say we have to climb the hill of passion
to get to a city of god, to find rebirth in ashes.
Here an opossum's been trapped in a tree, as
a crowd gathers by a park at Lincoln Avenue.
It's a giant mouse, says a Haitian guy, a tot takes
out a slingshot to try to coax the critter down.
Birders gaze at a gasping clump of fur, forget

that they were counting orioles on a balcony.
Traffic is at a standstill at this sight, lindens
sag in sudden winds, our troupe of pilgrims
eyes a bashed-up Subaru by a rotting snag.
Somebody says there's a snake in a manhole,
maybe not a boa, maybe more an anaconda.
Benign neglect, wicked cold, mindless thinking:

we're tired, we want to take a train at Roosevelt.
We sit in the softest moss and count out nickels
for the never-ending fare of Indonesian noodles,
Greek kebabs, Irish corned beef, Polish blintzes,
Delhi curry, Oaxaca tacos with lime or jalapeño.
We meet near 52nd Street to swap our travel tips,
an actor asks if we can visit the Queens Museum.

61ST STREET—WOODSIDE

Planes fly low over this sky-high subway stop,
we can see whites of the eyes of a stewardess,
buckled in for landing at LaGuardia. She spies
a prison bus on the bridge to Rikers Island,
rows of coffins at the edge of a potter's field.
A bookstore is opening its roll-top doors, kids
selecting video games for their drive to Islip.

We get out and go down to a local beer hall,
near the chestnut tree once used in public
proclamations for the Revolutionary War.
Springs trickle runoff in what's left of a
skunk cabbage swamp, where a tow path
ran through mulberry trees to a dance hall.
A copper beech stands by bygone trolleys,

A Filipina girl, from Manila, takes pride
in a backyard flower patch for better days.
The fresh pond plank road's gone, it's now
the Brooklyn-Queens Expressway, limos
sailing over potholes and swollen asphalt.
Our group meets by a travel agency, heads
to Trains Meadow, the land of a rising sun.

69TH STREET—FISK AVENUE

We get off the train to see a sunset movie
on a rooftop, just as stars are coming out.
In 1930, a ride from Great Neck to the city
meant passing the Valley of the Ashes, its
piles of burning trash, like Dead Horse Bay
in Brooklyn, a dumpsite for depleted nags.
We get back on the subway at Fisk Street,

see a Shinnecock trapper, in town to claim
the land that once was streams for trout.
Here Martha Peterson, nearly 27-years old,
succumbed to deadly smallpox, she's found
now buried in an iron coffin. Field workers
from Quogue are loitering at a deli, while
a videographer makes films about a ride

on a Third Avenue Elevated in its heyday.
An express train rolls by on flyover tracks,
our local shunting off to the Corona yards.
In a backyard Thai café, we drink Laotian
beer with catfish and papaya, to celebrate
our liberty as we explore the boroughs, the
Shinnecock man still with us on the train.

74TH STREET—BROADWAY

In Jackson Heights, an alley smells of cardamom,
pony-tailed sisters are wildly playing quena flutes.
We record them and share it with a nephew living
in Berlin, who, laughing, says he's seen them madly
drumming on the Ku'damm, their music travelling
in waves of loneliness or grief. I take our pilgrims
to a chateau, where gardeners weed a meadow rue.

We meet Eddy, a grizzled old greyhound, a race-
track veteran, his eyes are glazed with utter joy.
Some of us try on saris, savor tandoori chicken,
check in where you can buy a home in La Paz
for next to nothing. Farsi poets sit with cosmic
wheels and crosswords. We used to take a bus
from here to Jamaica Bay to walk, watch owls

and the far-off projects in East New York. Coots,
cranes, a coconut husk washed up on the shore.
This is station stop fourteen, station of the cross
where you can watch a hundred football games.
Near Roosevelt, we cup our ears, an ice cream
truck backfires, cars honk, a train above us roars.
In Jackson Heights, discos have replaced the ponds.

82ND STREET—JACKSON HEIGHTS

We've lost members of our group to chest colds,
one with a colicky ten-month old with blue eyes
like the sea, as we go on to Junction Boulevard,
recalling walks in search of no one can say what,
from volcanoes to mausoleums and mountains,
to making a pilgrimage to moon or star or tree,
in the middle of the arctic or up a city's avenues.

Why the urge to journey far from home? Maybe
to learn, to shout, undo, reframe, enjoy or smile.
Some say it's a process of un-selving, letting ego
go, listening to whispers, letting words flow.
I walk to St. Marks Church, where worshippers
intone "I thirst," much like how I start a poem,
startling a feeling into the shape of an eruption.

I stroll to Northern Boulevard, once a carriage
road for ladies, see the Freedom Tower's spires.
It makes me feel like listing things I love: corn
fields, broken noses, coffee cups, bloody eyes,
rhino tusks, horse hair, hoary bats, cellar doors,
moths, uninvited mice, you get my point if you
are reading this, but I've lost my train of thought.

90TH STREET—ELMHURST AVENUE

Known for Newtown apples, flower shops, tea
stands, a temple elephant, a church for mountain
climbers, it's what our Cuban sociologist refers
to as petit bourgeois, a community that dreams
of bridal veils, bocce, bar mitzvahs, dragon boats
and a festival of colors. The creek beds hosted
Hoovervilles, a blight that continues on today.

Once big gas tanks could be seen from the LIE,
answering a kid's eternal cry: *Are We There Yet?*
This is an urban zone with bus stops, strip malls
and Trader Joes, Home Depot, fenced-in yards
and cookie-cutter homes that whisper quietly.
Skunks, starlings, occasional spiny porcupines
straddle the greening belt between three worlds.

We search for the neighborhood of Lena Horne,
noticing every name that masks the strain of
poverty and crime: Kew Gardens, Floral Park.
In Elmhurst, Malcolm X brought up his girls,
a man in search of truth to build up civil rights,
his house bombed in 1965, before he lost his life.
On the sidewalk, a man is selling mosque clocks.

JUNCTION BOULEVARD

I drift into daydream as we exit Elmhurst,
channel Neil Young on his Greendale tour,
my family sitting on a grassy hillside, three
of us just enjoying a stress-free day together.
Junction Boulevard reveals a sunken house
of worship, a busy squat, 'hood hoops, lilies.
We meander past a Tiffany furnace works

where Byzantine glass and lapis lazuli are
used in high-tea cups. By a salumeria, we
hear steel-drum calypso at set-back single
homes forgotten by many mayors. Train-
spotters come: Lucien, who's ten, counts
the car types that rest at the bottom of
a reef in Slaughter Bay, where worn-out

models go to die with army tanks, barges,
a ton of tires in greenish waters that are
home to barnacles, spider crabs and squid.
At our stop we meet Olivia, who's writing
of *carusi* boys from sulfur mines in Sicily:
our herpetologist is moved, says he'll tune
up his search for chorus frogs in Queens.

for Dorothy Schmiderer Baker

103RD STREET—CORONA

Ribbons of white plasma issue from the surface
of the sun, its corona, changing shape and size.
Louis Armstrong lived on 107th Street, playing
Storyville, San Francisco, Quebec, Cameroon
and Congo. His smile, his style, his giant heart
and rasping voice put joy into jazz. He charmed
children on his stoop, as well as Marilyn and JFK

and the King of Thailand (playing on the sax).
"Meet Me in Paris" floods from his bedroom,
a turntable spins his song of beans and rice.
We sit in a garden as honeysuckle blooms,
robins time their worm jabs to his melodies,
all of us uplifted by his cheery lilt, as ghosts
of Ellington, Ella, usher in. I close my eyes

and hear his "Melancholy Blues" as it soars
into space with the Voyager space probe,
together with Bach, bagpipes, shakuhachi,
Plutonic odes, images of nursing mothers,
a spiral sketch of dancing sperm and ovum.
Reeling off in ether, 100 million miles away,
it's Satchmo's blues that help us journey on.

111TH STREET

Bjork's busy conducting humpback whales
at the Hall of Science in Flushing Meadows,
where rockets go to die, no more blasting off
to outer space for mining crater dust on Mars.
I take a photo of my daughter, a giant globe
as backdrop, her thoughts are very far away.
A Trylon and a Perisphere stood here for

the first World's Fair, a nod to engineers
who rebuilt factories from the inside out.
Superman was there as well as color film,
a talking, smoking robot named Elektro,
a merry-go-round for milk cows, a town
of tomorrow, a time capsule for 6939.
Here the UN met to partition the Holy

Land, its orange groves and olive trees.
I love Guston's worker murals, signaling
a return to public works or peace through
understanding, the theme of the next fair
my family visited when I was eight. There
were Belgian waffles, a Sinclair dinosaur,
a gloom in the car foreshadowing a divorce.

METS—WILLETS POINT

The hazy blocks between Citi Field and the bay
don't have sidewalks or sewers, just palsied dogs
who are yelping at the stars. Chop shops, car
parts, iron works in a triangle of track, puddles,
another world just minutes from a city's heart.
Sex shops, pimps, deadbeat dads asleep all day.
Two machinists, Rudi and Ali, pound hubcaps

into useful life as junkies stare. A single tenant,
like Timon of Athens, curses his enemies as he
doesn't want to leave his family home to make
way for House of Spices stores, shopping courts
that call to mind the Mall of Emirates, with Ski
Dubai, fountains and fireworks, its petting zoo.
Maybe a stadium for Maradona? A pushcart rolls

off a corrugated roof past barrels burning trash,
urine pools and yellowlegs wading in the creek.
This is an urban Land of Oddiyana. We don't
get off, we keep going to get to Main Street.
A man is gesturing at clouds beyond a patch
of peonies as wide as the eye can see, a good
locale here to detail your Lincoln Continental.

FLUSHING—MAIN STREET

I've reached the end, I don't know where to go.
I thank our guide, look for the weeping beech,
beehives in a botanical garden, a Paris bakery
and a *biang biang* noodle shop for hearing tales
from a middle kingdom, the South China Sea,
prophecies from Lao-tzu, a maze of terracotta
soldiers in a land of sprouting factory towns,

electric cars and ghost-like, skyscraper cities.
Roads here lead to a remonstrance, a religious
plea to Peter Stuyvesant allowing silent worship.
We sip tea at an Afghan eatery, where we meet
our final penitent, a mom returned from war.
She recalls a memory of vanishing, and cheery
children, rolling hoops and skipping stones

off a pontoon bridge on the Kabul River. I sit
by a bustling music school, the bus stop for
the Bronx and a tattoo shop, wondering how
we survived the human bottleneck, here now
chasing butterflies in Flushing. As a finishing
touch, I daub a brushstroke on a painted sign,
I add one dot to punctuate my final sentence.

for Arthur Smith, 1913-1999

22 STATIONS (CODA TO 21 STATIONS)

I'm sitting in Brooklyn's Shakespeare Garden,
listening to an ancient erhu. Far from Queens,
I wonder how to adjust my 21, 21-line poems
of the stations of the 7 train, to a 22nd stop
just built at Hudson Yards, sprouting out of
tunnels for the poor like mushroom spores
and native plants up on the High Line. But

the teardrop subway stop has burst apart
the underground, where my friend from
Budapest and I would roam the West Side
piers, eating enchiladas at a west side diner.
We combed the streets for hand-me-downs
and walked for miles as there was no train.
The subway stop, built for 2012 Olympics

that never came to be, is a go-to in itself.
It's raining here, and in a park downtown
in Saint-Denis, Réunion, where another
friend is introducing a bill on climate
change to government. It's also pouring
at the 34th St-Hudson Yards station, across
the river, end of the line for our tomorrow.

NOTES

Bannister's Landscapes
Edward Mitchell Bannister was among the earliest Rhode Island landscape painters, the first African American artist to win national recognition, and a founding member of the Providence Art Club. His landscapes showed the influence of the Barbizon style, an awareness of the Hudson River School, and the developing Impressionist movement. He was an active member of Providence public life as well as an accomplished and well-known painter.

The poet found a list of painting titles in an attic archive. Most of the paintings no longer exist. The project of these poems was to recreate the landscapes that are lost to history. The titles of his landscapes create a simple and beautiful narrative that underscores a need to "capture" the disappearing agrarian life of Southern New England but also recognize the growth of cities and industry. For the booming mills that changed the face of 19th century life throbbed just upriver from his favorite ponds and pastures.

His work was steeped in a Romantic spirit and an emotional response to nature. Bannister's words provide a link between his private vision and the streets of bustling Providence, the Art Club, and the soon-to-be Pen and Pencil Club. They provide a gloss on his bucolic scenes of harmony and quiet. Bannister was not a wordsmith, but his paintings' titles tell a story.

The Largest Glue Factory in the World
These poems look at the smells, sights, sounds of mid-nineteenth century America, in New York (around Newtown Creek, Brooklyn) as well as the life and times of Peter Cooper, at once educator, inventor, abolitionist and candidate for the U.S. Presidency, pre-Gilded Age self-made man, but also a grand polluter of the New York waterways.

The 14, 14-line poems use a loose sonnet form, and echo the Persian ghazal with an emphasis on the smelly things people pass by every day, living in the city.

Crossing Queensbridge

Hart Crane's "The Bridge" is magnificent and carries Whitman's "Crossing Brooklyn Ferry" into modernist times for Brooklyn. So here at the 150th anniversary of the Queensboro Bridge is a take on its idleness, industry and idiosyncrasies.

21 Stations

"21 Stations" evokes lives and music and history along the 21 stations of the 7 train, the 167 languages spoken there, journeying east out of the city. The poem is inspired by Awkafina and Chaucer's *The Canterbury Tales*. This piece formally was a set of 21, 21-line poems, which the poet calls sonnets-and-a-half. It is about the patchwork quilt of culture across Queens as seen in the river of commerce, reflection and imagination of the 7 train.

Thirty pilgrims set out from Times Square to wend their ways to the Weeping Beech in Chinatown, in Flushing, where bats can still be seen in belfries. Over the course of writing this series, they added a station at Hudson Yards, making it the uneven "22." The poem "22 Stations (Coda to 21 Stations)" addresses this.

The poet says that as he took the subway daily he'd look back at a completed poem and note that it took exactly the same time to read it out loud as it took to travel from one stop to the next.

ACKNOWLEDGEMENTS

Poems Published
"Crossing Queensbridge," published in "Alligatorzine," 166, 2016

Special Thanks
Special thanks goes to Barbara Westermann, Lotte Marie Allen, Devek Singh, Norman MacAfee, Marjory Wentworth, Michael Dinwiddie, Ken Miller, Brian Burt, Robert Bedick, Mark Patsfall, Jochen Saueracker, Emily Knight as well as Patricia Spears Jones and Kimiko Hahn from the days of poetry brigades against U.S. intervention in Latin America.

About the Author
Bill's work echoes beloved voices from poetry, poets, history and politics and a new look at nature in an era of climate action, with personal memories and a look into language, love and the ties that bind us together. There's humor, humanism, a music of the earth, a quest for ethical answers in a world titling off its axis. Inspired by Lowell and Bishop, Frank O'Hara and Ashbery, Pier Paolo Pasolini, Philip Levine and Muriel Rukeyser's spirit of questioning and grace.

He is the recipient of a 2009 National Endowment for the Arts fellowship in Creative Writing and has published three books of poems, *The Man on the Moon* (New York University and Persea Presses, 1987), *Sevastopol: On Photographs of War* (Xenos Press, 1997) and *North Passage* (Clay Street Press, 2019). His work can be seen at www.ekphrases.com.

He has been working at the United Nations in New York for over 15 years and hopes to bring humanism and heart to the poetry canon. He's currently working with the Red Hook Conservation Advisory Council to explore and protect the natural resources of the Hudson River Valley where he lives with the artist Barbara Westermann.

www.ingramcontent.com/pod-product-compliance
Lightning Source LLC
Chambersburg PA
CBHW031245120626
46545CB00007B/2653